W9-BZT-227

This book
belongs to:

....

....

The Colors of the Rainbow

Text: **Jennifer Moore-Mallinos**

Illustrations: **Marta Fàbrega**

BARRON'S

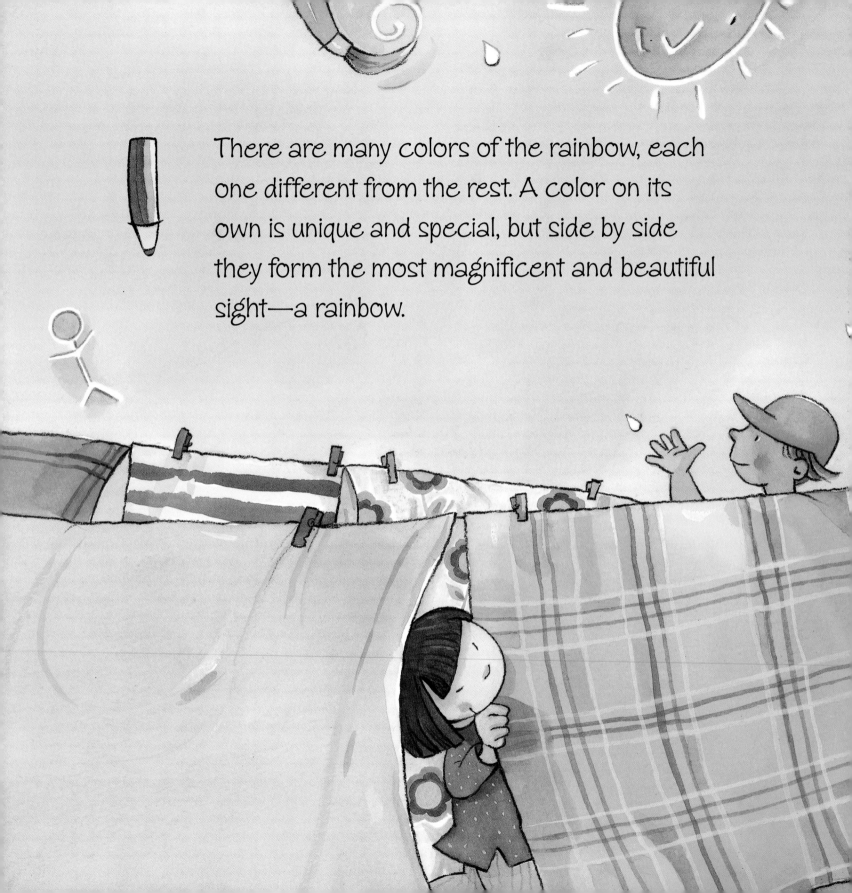

There are many colors of the rainbow, each one different from the rest. A color on its own is unique and special, but side by side they form the most magnificent and beautiful sight—a rainbow.

Just like the colors of the rainbow, people are unique in their own special way. When people from all around the world come together, they form a sight that is as lovely as a rainbow.

Although people may seem different on the outside, they are all the same on the inside. Our skin has many colors and shades.

Some of us have dark skin and some have light skin. Some skins get nice suntans whereas others get sunburns. But no matter how different our skin may appear, we all have beautiful shades of skin.

Our hair comes in all shapes and lengths, colors and shades. Hair may be black, brown, red, blonde, and many shades of those colors. Some hair is curly and some is straight. No matter how different our hair may be, short or long, dark or light, braided or in ponytails, we all have beautiful, colorful hair.

While our eyes may look different, we all have two, which allow us to see.

Some people have round eyes and some have narrow eyes; some eyes are big and some are small. Some people have dark brown eyes and some have light brown eyes. Other people have blue eyes and even green.

We all wear different clothes. Some people wear blue jeans, some people wear saris, and some wear burkas, but we all wear clothes. Clothes not only help us to keep warm, but they also tell a story of who we are or even where we are from.

 Each of us is unique by the language we speak. Many people speak English, but many others speak Chinese, Spanish, or Arabic.

Some people speak more than one language, but we all use language to communicate. Even when we don't understand what others are saying, we all understand what a smile means. So, let's all smile!

We also eat different foods. Some people like to eat pizza, but others prefer fried rice. Some of us like to eat pirogi, while others prefer curried chicken. There are many different kinds of food, and trying something new is always fun, even if it's different from what we're used to eating.

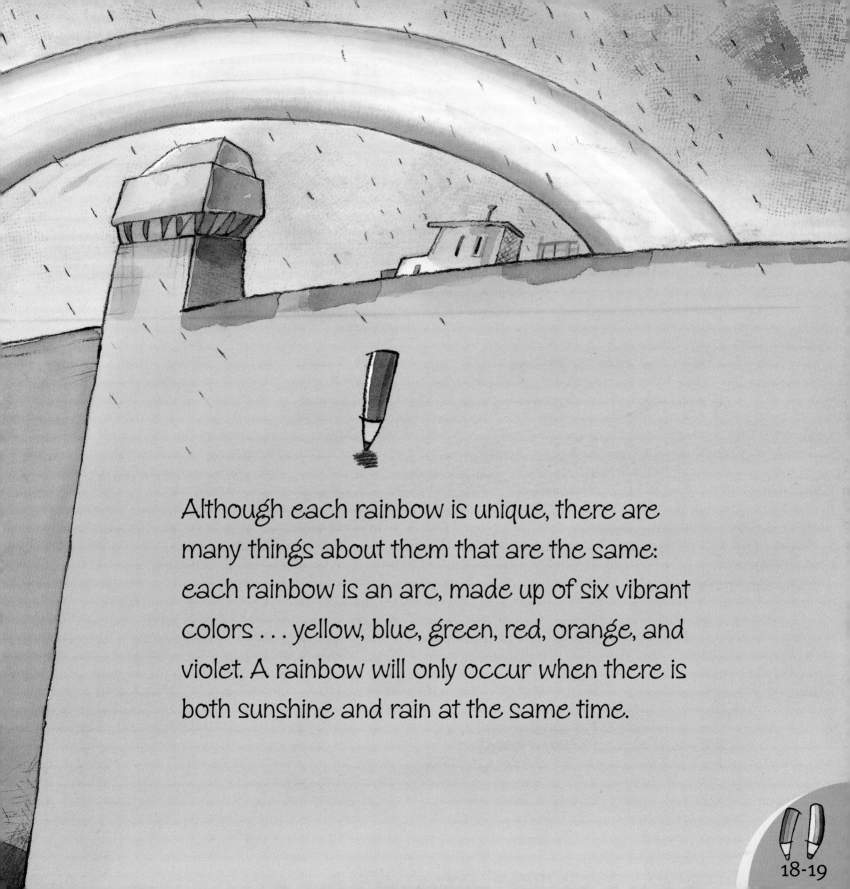

Although each rainbow is unique, there are many things about them that are the same: each rainbow is an arc, made up of six vibrant colors . . . yellow, blue, green, red, orange, and violet. A rainbow will only occur when there is both sunshine and rain at the same time.

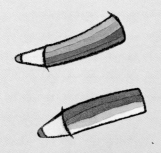

People are unique in their own special way, but just like a rainbow, we all have many things in common: we feel happiness and sadness, love and pain. When we are happy, we may smile, and when we are sad, we may cry. If we fall down, we feel pain. If we have a nightmare, we feel scared, and when we get a hug from someone special, we feel love.

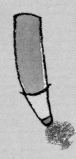

We each have a family who
loves and takes care of us
and a place we call home.
Our families and homes may
look very different on the
outside, but on the inside,
they give us love, warmth,
and make us feel safe.
There's no better place
than home!

We all enjoy spending time with our friends by playing games like skipping, marbles, hopscotch, or hide and seek. It really doesn't matter who we are or where we live: we all want to have fun and to be with our friends while we grow up.

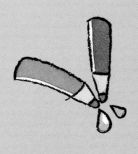

We all like to celebrate
special days that bring our
families and friends together.
A special day may be a
birthday, or Christmas,
Ramadan, or Hanukkah.
Whatever the occasion,
special days bring meaning
and togetherness into all of
our lives. Let's celebrate!

We have seen that just like a rainbow, we are both unique and similar in our own special way. We all have skin, hair, and eyes. We all wear clothes, use language to communicate, and eat food. We all have feelings, thoughts, hopes, and dreams. When we get hurt we cry, and when we are happy we laugh. When we are young, we dream about the future, and when we are old, we dream about the past.

Let's celebrate our differences!
Let's appreciate our uniqueness!
Let's come together and build a rainbow!

28-29

Note
to Parents

We live in a world of great diversity where people from everywhere come together to build communities and to raise their families. Being adults, we know that although people may appear very different on the outside, we are actually more the same than we are different.

There are many colors of the rainbow, each color different from the rest. Every color is unique and special, but side by side they form a truly wonderful sight.

The purpose of *The Colors of the Rainbow* is to acknowledge our differences, while at the same time recognizing that there are many things about each of us that are the same. By accepting people for who they are and by appreciating their differences, we take the first step toward achieving harmony.

The Colors of the Rainbow can be used as a tool to initiate dialogue and stimulate communication between you and your child. With your help, your child will have the opportunity to notice the many differences among people while also realizing that people are more alike than they seem.

Let's celebrate our differences, appreciate our uniqueness, and come together to build a rainbow! Diversity is our strength, not our weakness!

Taking the time to read to your child is a wonderful way to share a moment together. Children are our future. What they think and how they feel matters. Our children will someday determine how cultures can come together in peace and harmony.

Let's show our children that we truly care!

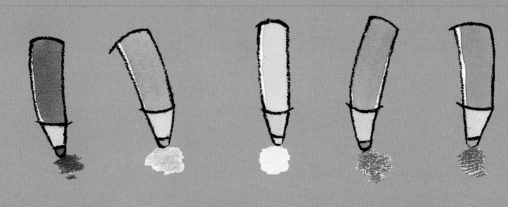

THE COLORS OF THE RAINBOW

First edition for the United States and Canada published in
2005 by Barron's Educational Series, Inc.
Original title of the book in Spanish: *Los Colores del Arco Iris*.
© Copyright 2005 by Gemser Publications, S.L.
El Castell, 38; Teià (08329) Barcelona, Spain (World Rights)
Author: Jennifer Moore-Mallinos
Illustrations: Marta Fàbrega

All inquiries should be addressed to:
Barron's Educational Series, Inc.
250 Wireless Boulevard
Hauppauge, New York 11788
http://www.barronseduc.com

ISBN-13: 978-0-7641-3277-3
ISBN-10: 0-7641-3277-6
Library of Congress Control Number 2005926576

Printed in China
9 8 7 6 5 4 3 2 1